To:

From:

The Best of
brain droppings

GEORGE CARLIN

PETER PAUPER PRESS, INC.
WHITE PLAINS, NEW YORK

The text in this book was excerpted from
Braindroppings by George Carlin, originally
published in paperback by Hyperion in 1997. This
edition published by arrangement with Hyperion.

Peter Pauper Press, Inc.
202 Mamaroneck Avenue
White Plains, NY 10601
All rights reserved
ISBN 978-1-59359-874-7

7 6 5 4 3 2 1

Visit us at www.peterpauper.com

The Best of
brain droppings

PREFACE

For a long time, my stand-up material has drawn from three sources. The first is the English language: words, phrases, sayings, and the ways we speak. The second source, as with most comedians, has been what I think of as the "little world," those things we all experience every day: driving, food, pets, relationships, and idle thoughts. The third area is what I call the "big world": war, politics, race, death, and social issues. Without having actually measured, I would say this book reflects that balance very closely.

If you read something in this book that sounds like advocacy of a particular political point of view, please reject the notion. My interest in "issues" is merely to point out how badly we're doing, not to suggest a way we might do better. Don't confuse me with those who cling to hope. I enjoy describing how things are, I have no interest in how they "ought to be." And I certainly have no interest in fixing them. I sincerely believe that if you think there's a solution, you're part of the problem.

P. S. Lest you wonder, personally, I am a joyful individual with a long, happy marriage and a close and loving family. My career has turned out better than I ever dreamed, and it continues to expand. I am a personal optimist but a skeptic about all else. What may sound to some like anger is really nothing more than sympathetic contempt. I view my species with a combination of wonder and pity, and I root for its destruction. And please don't confuse my point of view with cynicism; the real cynics are the ones who tell you everything's gonna be all right.

PEOPLE WHO SHOULD BE PHASED OUT

✘ Guys who always harmonize the last few notes of "Happy Birthday."

✘ Guys who wink when they're kidding.

✘ Men who propose marriage on the giant TV screen at a sports stadium.

✘ Guys in their fifties who flash me the peace sign and really mean it.

✘ Guys with creases in their jeans.

✗ People who know a lot of prayers by heart.

✗ A celebrity couple who adopt a Third-World baby and call it Rain Forest.

✗ Guys who wear suits all day and think an earring makes them cool at night.

✗ Men who have one long, uninterrupted eyebrow.

✗ Guys who wink and give me the peace sign simultaneously.

✗ Fat guys who laugh at everything.

✗ People who give their house or car a name.

✘ People who give their genitals a name.

✘ Guys who can juggle, but only a little bit.

✘ Men who wear loafers without socks. Especially if they have creases in their jeans.

✘ Guys who still smell like their soap in the late afternoon.

✘ Guys who wear their watches on the inside of their wrists.

✘ Guys who flash me the thumbs-up sign. Especially if they're winking and making the peace sign with the other hand.

A FEW THINGS I LIKE

● A guy who doesn't know what he's doing and won't admit it.

● A permanently disfigured gun collector.

● A whole lotta people tap dancing at once.

● When a big hole opens up in the ground.

● The third week in February.

● Guys who say "cock-a-roach."

● A woman with no feet, because she's not always nagging you to take her dancing.

I'M TIRED OF ...

... reading about clouds in a book. Doesn't this piss you off? You're reading a nice story, and suddenly the writer has to stop and describe the clouds. Who cares? I'll bet you anything I can write a decent novel, with a good, entertaining story, and never once mention the clouds. Really! Every book you read, if there's an outdoor scene, an open window, or even a door slightly ajar, the writer has to say, "As Bo and Velma walked along the shore, the clouds hung ponderously on the horizon like steel-gray, loosely formed gorilla turds." I'm not interested. Skip the clouds and get to the fucking. The only story I know of where clouds were important was Noah's Ark.

KEEP IT CLEAN

I never wash my hands after using a public restroom. Unless something gets on me. Otherwise, I figure I'm as clean as when I walked in. Besides, the sink is usually filthier than I am. I'm convinced that many of the men I see frantically washing up do not do the same thing at home. Americans are obsessed with appearances and have an unhealthy fixation on cleanliness. Relax, boys. It's only your dick. If it's so dirty that after handling it you need to wash your hands, you may as well just go ahead and scrub your dick while you're at it. Tell the truth. Wouldn't you like to see some guy trying to dry his genitals with one of those forced-air blowing machines that are mounted four feet off the ground?

G.C.'S GUIDE TO DINING OUT

RESTAURANTS

There are certain clues that tell you how much a restaurant will cost. If the word *cuisine* appears in the advertising, it will be expensive. If they use the word *food*, it will be moderately priced. However, if the sign says *eats*, even though you'll save some money on food, your medical bills may be quite high.

I don't like trendy food. When I hear, "sautéed boneless panda groin," I know I'm in the wrong place. There's such a thing as pretentious food. Puree of woodchuck, marinated bat nipples, weasel chops, porcupine cacciatore. Or fried eagle. A guy said to me recently, "C'mon, we'll go to Baxter's, they have really great fried eagle." I'm thinkin' to myself, "Do I really wanna know this guy?"

DEALING WITH THE WAITER

I think when you eat out you should have a little fun; it's good for digestion. Simple things. After the waiter recites a long list of specials, ask him if they serve cow feet.

Have fun. Be difficult. Order unusual things: a chopped corn sandwich. Rye potato chips. Filet of bone with diced peas. Peanut butter and jellyfish. Ask for a glass of skim water. Insist on fried milk. Chocolate orange juice. Order a grilled gorgonzola cheese sandwich on whole-wheat ladyfingers. Then top the whole thing off with a bowl of food coloring and a large glass of saturated fat.

If they have a salad bar, ask how many times you can go back. If they say as many times as you like, ask for a lawn bag. Come back the next day with a small truck. Tell them you weren't quite finished eating the night before. You're actually within your legal rights, because, technically, no one is ever finished eating.

FOOD TERMS

BREADSTICKS:

If drumsticks are for playing drums, you'd think breadsticks would be for playing bread, wouldn't you? "Would you like some bread-sticks?" "No thank you. I don't play bread; I play drums. Perhaps I'll have a drum roll."

SHELLED PEANUTS:

Why don't shelled peanuts have shells? If you're clothed, you have clothes, so if you're shelled, you should have shells. You'd think they'd call peanuts without shells, "unshelled" peanuts, wouldn't you? Same goes for pitted prunes.

And boned chicken. I ask you, Where are the bones? I can't find them. In my opinion, it ought to be called *de*-boned chicken.

WAFFLE IRON:

Why on earth would you want to iron a waffle? Wouldn't that just flatten out all the little squares? No, I believe waffles should be dry cleaned. Pancakes, of course, should always be ironed.

GOBBLE THIS

On Thanksgiving at our house we like variety, so we don't have turkey every year. Last year we had a swan. It was nice; everyone got some neck. Another year we had a seagull. Delicious! It's a little fishy, but at least there's no need to add salt. Two years ago we had a stork. Lots of meat, but, Jesus, the wishbone makes a helluva noise. This year we're expecting a few people over, so we're having a flamingo. And I'm getting the leg that folds up. They say the meat is sweeter and more tender because the flamingo doesn't use it much.

SUN OF GOD

I've begun worshipping the sun for a number of reasons. First of all, unlike some other gods I could mention, I can see the sun. It's there for me every day. And the things it brings me are quite apparent all the time: heat, light, food, a lovely day. There's no mystery, no one asks for money, I don't have to dress up, and there's no boring pageantry. And interestingly enough, I have found that the prayers I offer to the sun and the prayers I formerly offered to "God" are all answered at about the same 50-percent rate.

SMALL TOWNS

You know you're in a small town when:

✗ The restaurant closes at lunch so the waitress can go home and eat.

✗ The mayor's nickname is "Greasy Dick" and besides appearing on the ballot, it also appears on his driver's license.

✗ The fashion boutique/post office is located in one corner of the hardware store between the used milking machines and the pay toilet.

✘ The police station is closed evenings and weekends, but they leave lit the sign that gives the time and temperature.

✘ The newspaper prints the crossword puzzle on the front page above the fold, and prints the answers just below.

✘ The zip code has three digits and features a decimal point.

✘ The Narcotics Anonymous chapter has only one member, and he's strung out on ranch dressing.

TALKING AND LISTENING

You know how sometimes, at a busy cocktail party, when you're telling a group of people a story, a few of them may become distracted, and you lose their attention? So you concentrate a little harder on the ones who are still listening? You know that feeling? And then, because it's a lively party, a few more of them drift away? And as your audience slowly peels off one by one, after a while you wind up addressing any person you can find who's willing to look at you. Even the busboy. And then you realize the busboy doesn't understand English. Isn't that awful?

Sometimes, a person some distance away from you will say something you can't quite understand, so you ask them to repeat it, and you still can't make it out. You try two or three more times without any luck, and by then you're getting embarrassed, so you pretend to understand, and just say, "Yeah!" so you can be done with it. Later, it turns out they said, "We're coming over tonight to remove your wife's ovaries. Will that be all right?"

Z-Z-Z-Z-Z-Z-Z-Z-Z

People say, "I'm going to sleep now," as if it were nothing. But it's really a bizarre activity. "For the next several hours, while the sun is gone, I'm going to become unconscious, temporarily losing command over everything I know and understand. When the sun returns, I will resume my life."

If you didn't know what sleep was, and you had only seen it in a science fiction movie, you would think it was weird and tell all your friends about the movie you'd seen.

"They had these people, you know? And they would walk around all day and be OK? And then, once a day, usually after dark, they would lie down on these special platforms and become unconscious. They would stop functioning almost completely, except deep in their minds they would have adventures and experiences that were completely impossible in real life. As they lay there, completely vulnerable to their enemies, their only movements were to occasionally shift from one position to another; or, if one of the 'mind adventures' got too real, they would sit up and scream and be glad they weren't unconscious anymore. Then they would drink a lot of coffee."

So, next time you see someone sleeping, make believe you're in a science fiction movie. And whisper, "The creature is regenerating itself."

BASEBALL AND FOOTBALL

Baseball is different from any other sport; very different.

For instance, in most sports you score points or goals; in baseball you score runs.

In most sports the ball, or object, is put in play by the offensive team; in baseball the defensive team puts the ball in play, and only the defense is allowed to touch the ball. In fact, in baseball if an offensive player touches the ball intentionally, he's out; sometimes unintentionally, he's out.

Also: In football, basketball, soccer, volleyball, and all sports played with a ball, you score *with* the ball, and without the ball you can't score. In baseball the ball prevents you from scoring.

In most sports the team is run by a coach; in baseball the team is run by a manager; and only in baseball does the manager (or coach) wear the same clothing the players do. If you had ever seen John Madden in his Oakland Raiders football uniform, you would know the reason for this custom.

Now, I've mentioned football. Baseball and football are the two most popular spectator sports in this country. And, as such, it seems they ought to be able to tell us something about ourselves and our values. And maybe how those values have changed over the last 150 years. For those reasons, I enjoy comparing baseball and football:

◊ Baseball is a nineteenth-century pastoral game.
Football is a twentieth-century technological struggle.

◊ Baseball is played on a diamond, in a park. The baseball park!
Football is played on a gridiron, in a stadium, sometimes called Soldier Field or War Memorial Stadium.

◊ Baseball begins in the spring, the season of new life.
Football begins in the fall, when everything is dying.

◊ In football you wear a helmet.
In baseball you wear a cap.

◊ Football is concerned with *downs*. "What down is it?"

Baseball is concerned with *ups*.
"Who's up? Are you up? I'm not up!
He's up!"

⬥ In football you receive a penalty.
In baseball you make an error.

⬥ In football the specialist comes in
to kick.
In baseball the specialist comes in
to relieve somebody.

⬥ Football has hitting, clipping, spear-
ing, piling on, personal fouls, late
hitting, and unnecessary roughness.
Baseball has the sacrifice.

◊ Football is played in any kind of weather: Rain, snow, sleet, hail, fog ... can't see the game, don't know if there is a game going on; mud on the field ... can't read the uniforms, can't read the yard markers, the struggle will continue!
In baseball if it rains, we don't go out to play. "I can't go out! It's raining out!"

◊ Baseball has the seventh-inning stretch.
Football has the two-minute warning.

◊ Baseball has no time limit: "We

don't know when it's gonna end!"
Football is rigidly timed, and it will
end "even if we have to go to sud-
den death."

In baseball, during the game, in
the stands, there's a kind of picnic
feeling. Emotions may run high or
low, but there's not that much
unpleasantness.
In football, during the game in the
stands, you can be sure that at least
twenty-seven times you were
perfectly capable of taking the life
of a fellow human being.

And finally, the objectives of the two games are completely different:

In football the object is for the quarterback, otherwise known as the field general, to be on target with his aerial assault, riddling the defense by hitting his receivers with deadly accuracy in spite of the blitz, even if he has to use the shotgun. With short bullet passes and long bombs, he marches his troops into enemy territory, balancing this aerial assault with a sustained ground attack that punches holes in the forward wall of the enemy's defensive line.

In baseball the object is to go home! And to be safe! "I hope I'll be safe at home!"

GOOD FOR HEADACHES

Sometimes on television they tell you a product is "good for headaches." I don't want something that's good for headaches. I want something that's bad for headaches. And good for me.

FUCK YOU, I LIKE THESE KINDS OF JOKES!

Chess: The piece movement.

Seersucker: A person who blows clairvoyants.

Outspoken: When you lose a debate.

Hormone: The sound a prostitute makes so you'll think you're a real good fuck.

Parakeet: A keet that takes care of you until the real keet arrives.

Beer nuts: The official disease of Milwaukee.

Cotton balls: The final stage of beer nuts.

Cowhand: An occupational disability common among dairy farmers.

Woodpecker: A seventeenth-century prosthetic device.

Leatherette: A short sadomasochist.

A gay barbarian: Attila the hon.

SIGNS

I have a suggestion that I think would help fight serious crime. Signs. There are lots of signs for minor infractions: No Smoking, Stay Off the Grass, Keep Out, and they seem to work fairly well. I think we should also have signs for major crimes: Murder Strictly Prohibited, No Raping People, Thank You for Not Kidnapping Anyone. It's certainly worth a try. I'm convinced Watergate would never have happened if there had just been a sign in the Oval Office that said, Malfeasance of Office Is

Strictly Against the Law, or Thank You for Not Undermining the Constitution.

When you drive through an entrance or exit lane that has one of those signs, Do Not Back Up—Severe Tire Damage, and you're going in the correct direction, don't you sort of worry about it anyway? That maybe they got it wrong? Or somebody turned the sign around? Or some guy on drugs installed the spikes? Or maybe *you're* on drugs, and you think, Am I doing this right? Am I backing up? No, I seem to be going forward. Let's see. Which way are the spikes pointing? Oh, I can't see the spikes anymore. I guess I better back up a little.

THROW YOUR BACK OUT

Several months ago, a friend told me that when he was cleaning his garage he threw his back out. I told him it was probably overenthusiasm. Sometimes when you're cleaning, you get carried away and throw out something you intended to keep. The next time I ran into him he seemed to have learned his lesson. He had recently cleaned out his attic, but this time he didn't throw his back out. He gave it to Goodwill.

SHORT TAKES (Part 1)

The nicest thing about anything is not knowing what it is.

- I feel sorry for homeless gay people; they have no closet to come out of. In fact, I imagine if you *were* gay and homeless, you'd probably be glad just to *have* a closet.

- I've adopted a new lifestyle that doesn't require my presence. In fact, if I don't want to, I don't have to get out of bed at all, and I still get credit for a full day.

Some see the glass as half-empty, some see the glass as half-full. I see the glass as too big.

◗ My uncle thought he would clean up in dirt farming, but prices fell, and he took a real bath. Eventually, he washed his hands of the whole thing.

Kilometers are shorter than miles. Save gas, take your next trip in kilometers.

◗ I have as much authority as the Pope, I just don't have as many people who believe it.

When you find existing time on a parking meter, you should be able to add it to the end of your life. Minus the time you spent on hold.

I recently went to a new doctor and noticed he was located in something called the Professional Building. I felt better right away.

I don't have to tell you it goes without saying there are some things better left unsaid. I think that speaks for itself. The less said about it the better.

When someone is impatient and says, "I haven't got all day," I always wonder, How can that be? How can you not have all day?

Shouldn't a complimentary beverage tell you what a fine person you are?

The *mai tai* got its name when two Polynesian alcoholics got in a fight over some neckwear.

Environmentalists changed the word *jungle* to *rain forest*, because no one would give them money to save a jungle. Same with *swamps* and *wetlands*.

The other night I ate at a real nice family restaurant. Every table had an argument going.

When you close your eyes and rub real hard, do you see that checkerboard pattern?

When you sneeze, all the numbers in your head go up by one.

HOUSES AND HOMES

That thing you live in? Is it a house, or is it a home? Developers sell homes, but people buy houses.

Most people don't mind if you put 'em in a house. But under no circumstances do they want you to put 'em in a home. Unless it's a happy home. A happy home is not the same as a happy house. A happy house is one that's just been cleaned and painted. You'd be happy, too.

The madam Polly Adler once said, "A house is not a home." Of course, she meant a whorehouse is not a home. And it's not; no one would ever go to a whore home. Except a really old whore. That's where they go: The Old Whore's Home.

SOME FAVORITE OXYMORONS

- assistant supervisor
- new tradition
- original copy
- plastic glass
- uninvited guest
- highly depressed
- live recording
- authentic reproduction
- partial cease-fire

- limited lifetime guarantee
- **elevated subway**
- dry lake
- **true replica**
- forward lateral
- **standard options**
- mutual differences
- **nondairy creamer**
- open secret
- **resident alien**
- silent alarm

- sports sedan
- wireless cable
- mercy killing
- business ethics
- friendly fire
- genuine veneer
- death benefits
- holy war

T here are some liberties taken with speech that I think require intervention, if only for my own sake. I won't feel right if this chance goes by, and I keep my silence.

Strictly speaking, *celibate* does not mean not having sex, it means not being married. No wedding. The practice of refraining from sex is called *chastity* or *sexual abstinence*. No fucking. Priests don't take a vow of celibacy, they take a vow of chastity. Sometimes referred to as the "no-nookie clause."

And speaking of sex, the *Immaculate Conception* does not mean Jesus was conceived in the absence of sex. It means Mary was conceived without Original Sin. That's all it has ever meant. And according to the tabloids, Mary is apparently the only one who can make such a claim. The Jesus thing is called *virgin birth*.

NAME IT LIKE IT IS

The words *Fire Department* make it sound like they're the ones who are starting the fires, doesn't it? It should be called the "Extinguishing Department." We don't call the police the "Crime Department." Also, the "Bomb Squad" sounds like a terrorist gang. The same is true of *wrinkle cream*. Doesn't it sound like it causes wrinkles? And why would a doctor prescribe pain pills? I already *have* pain! I need relief pills!

FROZEN MEXICAN DINNER

Sometimes on television they tell you to buy a frozen Mexican dinner. Well, it sounds like a good idea, but actually, before you take him out to dinner, I should think it would be a good idea to bring him in the house and let him warm up a little. A frozen Mexican probably wouldn't be thinking mainly about food. By the way, isn't Mexico a warm-weather country?

DESERVING CHARITIES

For my part, I like to work quietly in the background, helping my preferred charities raise money. If you'd like to help too, here are just a few you might consider.

✗ St. Anthony's Shelter for the Recently All Right

✗ The Christian Haven for the Chronically Feisty

✗ The Committee to Keep Something-or-Other from Taking Place

✘ The Center for Research into the Heebie Jeebies

✘ Free Hats for Fat People

✘ The Task Force for Better Pancakes

✘ The Alliance of People Who Don't Know What's Next

✘ The Downtown Mission for the Permanently Disheveled

✘ The League of People Who Should Know Better

✘ The Brotherhood of Real Creeps

SOME FAVORITE REDUNDANCIES

- added bonus
- exactly right
- closed fist
- future potential
- inner core
- money-back refund
- seeing the sights
- true fact
- revert back
- safe haven
- prior history

- young children
- **time period**
- sum total
- **end result**
- temper tantrum
- **ferryboat**
- free gift
- **bare naked**
- combined total
- **unique individual**
- potential hazard
- **joint cooperation**

POPULAR BELIEFS

There are many popular beliefs rooted in familiar expressions and sayings that simply aren't true.

◆ Everything comes in threes.

Not true. In reality, everything comes in ones. Sometimes, when three "ones" come in a row, it seems like everything comes in threes. By the way, in medieval times it was widely believed that everything came in twenty-sixes. They were wrong, too. It just took them longer to recognize a pattern.

- ## People say when you die, you can't take it with you.

  Well, that depends on what it is. If it's your dark blue suit, you can certainly take it with you. In fact, not only can you take it with you, you can probably put some things in the pockets.

- ## You learn something new every day.

  Actually, you learn something old every day. Just because you just learned it doesn't mean it's new. Other people already knew it. Columbus is a good example of this.

● The sky's the limit.

Well, how can the sky be the limit? The sky never ends. What kind of a limit is that? The Earth is the limit. You dig a hole and what do you keep getting? More earth. The Earth's the limit.

● You get what you pay for.

Clearly this is not true. Have you been shopping lately? Only a naive person would believe that you get what you pay for. In point of fact, if you check your purchases carefully, you'll find that you get whatever they feel like giving you. And if corporations get any more powerful, you soon might not even get that.

◗ You can't have it both ways.

That depends on how intimately you know the other person. Maybe you can't have it both ways at once, but if you've got a little time, you can probably have it six or seven ways.

WATCH YOUR MOUTH

Beware of Aggravating Speakers

I am easily annoyed by people's speech habits, and I regard certain words and phrases as warnings to break off contact. In the interest of maintaining good mental health, I avoid the following people:

Those who can't resist saying, "God forbid" each time they mention the possibility of an accident or death, even though they don't believe in God.

People who say "God rest his soul" following the mention of a dead person, even if they hated the person and don't believe in God.

I also think we'd be better off if we could eliminate anyone who has a "can-do" attitude, or is referred to as "take-charge," "all-business," or "no-nonsense." Have these people sedated.

And let's lose these guys who think it's cute to say, "Ouch!" when someone delivers a small put-down.

COME BACK AND SEE US, HEAR?

I suppose it would be nice if reincarnation were a reality, but I have problems with the math. At some point, originally, there must have been a time when there were only two human beings. They both died, and presumably their souls were reincarnated into two other bodies. But that still leaves us with only two souls. We now have nearly six billion people on the planet. Where are all the extra souls coming from? Is someone printing up souls? Wouldn't that tend to lower their value?

SOMETHING'S MISSING

Why are there no B batteries? There aren't even any A batteries. In fact, it's almost as if they went out of their way to avoid A. They went straight to AA and AAA. Also, I never see any grade B milk, or type III audio cassettes. And there are no vitamins F, G, H, I, and J. Why? Why are certain airline seat numbers missing, and what ever became of the Boeing 717? And Chanel #4? And why are there hardly any brown running shoes? Or green flowers? I dare not even mention blue food.

ANIMAL INSTINCTS

At the start, let me say I am not an animal rights activist. I'm not comfortable with absolutes.

And I know that every time something eats, something else dies. I recognize the Earth is little more than a revolving buffet with weather. So, the idea of eating animals is fine with me, but is it really necessary to make things out of the parts we don't eat? We're the only species that does this. You never see a mongoose with snakeskin shoes. Or a lion walkin' around in a wildebeest hat. And how often do you run into plankton that have phytoplankton luggage?

And I think people have a lot of nerve locking up a tiger and charging four dollars to let a few thousand worthless humans shuffle past him every day. What a shitty thing to do. Humans must easily be the meanest species on Earth. Probably the only reason there are any tigers left is because they don't taste good.

SHORT TAKES (Part 2)

I only respect horoscopes that are specific: "Today, Neil Perleman, wearing tight-fitting wool knickers, will kill you on the crosstown bus."

Whenever I hear about a "peace-keeping force," I wonder, If they're so interested in peace, why do they use force?

A scary dream makes your heart beat faster. Why doesn't the part of your brain that controls your heartbeat realize that another part of your brain is making the whole thing up? Don't these people communicate?

◗ Why does *Filipino* start with an *F* and *Philippines* start with *Ph*?

How can a color be artificial? I look at red Jell-O, and it's just as red as it can be.

◗ In Rome, the emperor sat in a special part of the Coliseum known as the Caesarian section.

Why are there no recreational drugs taken in suppository form?

- It is now possible for a child to have five parents: sperm donor, egg donor, the surrogate mother who carries the fetus, and two adoptive parents. It renders the statement "He has his mother's eyes" rather meaningless.

I choose toilet paper through a process of elimination.

- I'm in favor of personal growth as long as it doesn't include malignant tumors.

- Once, at a school function, I received a dressing down for not dressing up.

No one can ever know for sure what a deserted area looks like.

♦ I was taken to the hospital for observation. I stayed several days, didn't observe anything, and left.

♦ A tree: First you chop it down, then you chop it up.

If a painting can be forged well enough to fool experts, why is the original so valuable?

KILLER COMIC

It goes without saying I'm not the only person who has noticed this, but I never got to spell it out my way before.

Comedy's nature has two sides. Everybody wants a good time and a couple of laughs, and of course, the comic wants to be known as a real funny guy. But the language of comedy is fairly grim and violent. It's filled with punch lines, gags, and slapstick. After all, what does a comic worry most about? Dying! He doesn't want to die.

"Jeez, I was dyin'. It was like death out there. Like a morgue. I really bombed."

Comics don't want to die, and they don't want to bomb. They want to go over with a bang. And be a real smash. And if everything works out, if they're successful and they make you laugh, they can say, "I killed 'em. I slaughtered those people, I knocked them dead."

And what phrases do we use when we talk about the comic? "He's a riot." "A real scream." "A rib-splitting knee-slapper." "My sides hurt." "My cheeks ache." "He broke me up, cracked me up, slayed me, fractured me, and had me in stitches." "I busted a gut." "I get a real kick out of that guy."

"Laugh? I thought I'd die."